The Beginning Is The End

Aria Rozo

First published in the United States of America by Aria Rozo

Tacoma, WA

Visit ariarozo.com to contact publisher for permission and find more information.

Publisher's Cataloging in Publication data

Name: Rozo, Aria, author.

Title: The beginning is the end / by Aria Rozo.

Description: First Edition | A warrior journeys through a war-torn land. | Includes index.

Identifiers: PCN 2016909161 | ISBN 978-0-9976736-2-3 (ebook) | ISBN 978-0-9976736-1-6 (hbk.) | ISBN 978-0-9976736-0-9 (pbk.)

Subjects: Poetry. | Self discovery. | Epic.

Classification: LCC PN1301-1333

To all who have wandered in The Garden

For the lost

Stay

TABLE OF CONTENTS

AFTERWORD

You are buried now

No prayer

No sound

Here I am.

The

Somewhere Beautiful

Eyes close
The body falls
The soul lingers
The heavens call

Did I ask for too much?
Did I have any at all?

The more I held, the more I lost
So I let go
Throw, this failed cause

My mind is ravaged
My passion engulfed

The world will keep spinning
Creation will continue existing
Even as the children lay weeping
And the shielded sing, cheering

Aria Rozo

Did the sound of bells ever haunt you?
The chimes of comfort remind you?

As you lay in your bed
You sleep among the dead

Sleep now
Tomorrow will come, when you wake

From ashes anew
Your eyes will open, once eschewed

History will pass, but it will come back

For the day next is only a chance
to try again the last dance

How I Wonder What You Are

Naked

I am alone

Brightly shining
Fire in the cold

I wait

Still

No one calls me home

How can I echo beyond these walls?
There is no sound
No rift to close

Aria Rozo

Will I be found?

I call out to the darkness
A silence ringing a silence
Unheard, still I propose

My brethren
They do not reach me now

Tell me
For my blinks I can only doubt

Have my eyes been open all this Time

Or do they see the truth Divine?

Four Fingers

Wrap my neck
Steal my breath

If we each have a song
What sound is it all

Unclear variation
Then clarity in noise

Choke me
You're already taken
My pride
My joys

My voice is nothing
Unheard echoes
Fading

Aria Rozo

Let me feel

Yes, I want to feel

Let me gaze upwards

Come
Pull me down

If I die
I want to die by you

My life is yours
Say anything
I'll nod

"My love, of course."

Well...

There is a well of wishes
Everyone smiled
For all came true
Their visions

Yet a boy said something different
And to his reflection
He descent

A world just like his
Only less

Then he understood.

Some are cursed

That some are blessed

Aria Rozo

The Halcyon Days

<u>Bear</u>

You came through rain
Wet, shivering
Strength you feign

I embraced you,
From where have you fled?
Come rest next to the warm fire
Our shed

The months pass, trees shake off golden dust
You grew just like the sun
Peeking over the horizon, to it we run

Playing in that forest our silent home
Away from the worries of a city
In solitude, not alone

Words said never
Rain fell, my cheeks wetter

Yet you, oh so gentle
Cheered me, my heart settle

Soon our paths diverge, time grows low
To separate worlds we must go

Though our union is broken, we are not alone
As we set out to claim our thrones

Lament not we will meet again
If not here, then in our Ascent

For this is only a temporary parting
Our bond is much more than our holding

Just as this White rain, the world, covers
Entirely so do our thoughts
Envelop the other

The Bakery

I came for the bread
At the start
Led by curiosity
My heart

Enamored by the scent
My lips moisten
Breads crinkle
I can taste them as I listen

Approaching the counter
I prepare to leave

Yet, 'ere I go, for a moment you speak
I look up
And stood still
Halted, the beat

Thankfully, I wake
Regain my senses
"Thank you."
I whisper my sentence.

Hurriedly, I go
Eager to eat

I bite and savor my blessing
My tongue knows Heaven
A sweet trespassing

I smile broadly
Rush!
Hide my face quickly!
Lest anyone pass
Chuckle as they see me
My face red flushed

Time passes
Oft I keep returning
But over time, the smells and tastes
Are not what pull me in

My purpose changed, just a little
For all greeted by your smile
Their troubles settle

Festival

Hustle and bustle
Excitement and anticipation
Preparing costumes is half the participation

Different masks and dresses
Colored lamps, magic lessons
Fire breathing dragons on pylons
Spring flowers, dandelion

Candy, baked bread, full of flair
People playing, guitars, musical chairs

Streets are crowded, laughter and chatter
All worries gone, tomorrow doesn't matter

The future is far, far beyond the ocean

Now we all watch, fireworks in the sky blossom

Kites fly, waving their wings
As cats run from dogs, tails spill our things

Balloons too numerous to count
Just as stars, twinkle
Knights show off their sparkled mount
None too simple

Dances, I pull you forward to
Twirl and twirl all night we two

In this festival the night sways away
Each one forever wanting to stay

The Calm

<u>Little Joy</u>

Your feet tap the floor
Raindrops on the ground

Your laughter, to your heart a door
Delight, a wave returning to shore

Honey, butter
The feel, your voice

Scent, wine drops
Leaf, evergreen choice

Your words sweet shelter
Pour like nectar from an orange petal

Never did your spirits lower
As you were hid in this white twisted tower
Full of windows, outside

Skies you could not reach
Yet The One did you bless,
And never beseech

Evermore you dance and leap
Faith strongly did you keep

Hush, silence embraced
The Sleep is only for a while

A life sated
No, two

I'm glad for you I
Still
Waited

If

My hair dances about me
I rise up the mountain road

In the early morning hue
I comb the cool morning due

In this carriage, I gaze at the sunrise
Pretend our Marriage, no smile missed

Your scent I imagine, plum and wood
Your face I remember, I smile to calm, soothe

What if...

The distance between us grows
Yet I feel a precious hold

Your breath, I miss
Life shared in kiss

A hand I reached out to keep
Warmth shared asleep

We stop, I must depart
A last look, taste tart, vision mist

What if...

Close

Close my eyes, I fade
Listen
The night, air cool, trees sway

Fire crackles, embers bade
Words gentle, your embrace, my shade

Notes travel, silence rings
Voices fly, words with broken wings

Stream water flows, paths composed
Valley cross, river rain
I breathe deeply
Tears upon my noise have lain

Your hand I grip
Warmth surrounds

Whisper the night sings
Calm, to this feeling sink

Here, outside
Comfort found
Morrow, the Ship sails
To Freedom I am bound

Promises
Hushed lies
Yet I believe

Faith, I won't resign

Breathe
Hear the waters
Take our sighs

These are not my tears
But the salt of the ocean
It has voice
It can hear

Each wave a sigh
Eyes also dry

Hear me then
Tears of the mother

Drown
So
Drown our Byes

Fading Echo

Waking

A hundred years have passed, it seems

Salt and water upon my cheek, dry
Wiped off gently, my mask, torn seams

The candle fire dances around me, asleep
Towards the open window I slip

The world has changed.

Winds blow

I notice
Your missing presence

Know this
To pass through the pane,
Your essence

I only wish for you
Have you, my message?

The world is no more
No life, no sound, no score

Fingers reach out to touch me yet fade
I question myself
Am I still sane?
Am I enough of your dimension?

How long have I lain?

Tyrant

The waves pound the shore
My heart beats upon my chest, the door

You whisper
I listen to the distance

Shimmering
Frustrated stillness

This ship rises and falls to the waters
My movement is taken
Motionless,
What am I,
After?

The winds, your salty breaths
I am Here now,
Alone
But I do not bow

The war is over
The world I bent

Now I must take back our Covers
The souls once sent

I sail away
Beyond the Seven

Return I must
To where creation kneaded

The origin,
Where Life was seeded

The Climb

The Last Man

To another tomorrow let us go
A familiar future we are to hold

Uncertainty is the way of life
We are all slaves to our strife

No matter the reaches of this universe
We will never be free of our curse

This ship now leaves the planet
His family cries and looks back at the hamlet

The ground, trash

The air, a thick blaze
Rain pours, eating metal
Upward the man gazed

May you find Peace
Never fight for the least
Forget not to care for your mother
Always love one another

They vanished beyond the skies
He slowly lowered his sights
Finished with his wait
He closed the final gate

<u>Promise</u>

Don't you look down upon me
I am strong
More than you can see

Stand behind me!
Do not fear. They will not harm us.

I will fight
I will protect you

Our mother is lost
Father is but a ghost

But I will stand
I promise

Your eyes beg, think this our last moment

Aria Rozo

Yet I will never say those three words
For I will never die from these Swords

Others may give their Breath
To wrest their loves from Death

But I will never die for you

I will never die.

For you.

Tired

I am tired

Tired of slumber

The clock turns
An eternal number

Wake

Wake me
Paralyzed

Disturb the still waters

Show me

Paradise

Aria Rozo

Sight of Flight

Oh, notice, would you, the seafarers fly

In their warmth, the air up high

Their gaze turned North, always forward

Prouder than I, never to join them, my gaze lowered

Still my eyes touch the sky their sight never captures

My soul soars,

Freedom enraptures

Aria Rozo

Fear of Death

Footsteps beat the ground

Let your Voice ring a thunderous sound

To the Peak o'er the horizon travel boldly

Let your strength be known, foretold broadly

Might now envelops you, crushing boulder

Yearning to carry this World upon its shoulder

Forged in Heavenly Anvil, Hellish Fire, Ancient Soot

Grip now your Hammer of Merciless Truth

With infinite Will, from Evil, extract confession

The Fear of Death

Resurrection

Aria Rozo

The Storm

<u>Gladiator</u>

Fingers tremble
I rise

The crowds, I hear
Voices cry

My daggers, their hilts
I cradle

The battlefield, I near
Chariots rumble

His face flashes
Through my mind

If I must, a hundred beasts I will face,
No matter the kind

Bloody dust
I breathe

Aria Rozo

As sunlight pours
The arena I meet

Gladiators lunge
At the giant demon

One stroke, all slain
The strongest even

It spots me
To it I run
Courage feigned

My heart is my armor

Blood rains.

Mask

The dust rises from the ground
As the boots of the hero downward pounds

From a heart full of hatred
She seeks only fight to be sated

Rivers of blood spilled, it matters not, red Earth
Memories burn hot, deep within her Hearth

Cower and run, say the wise
As Ancient evil once more rise

Armies summoned to fight and die
Strewn upon the field, bodies lie

Her presence drives enemies to retreat
Yet her tiny silhouette is all to see

What is her essence, save to elicit laughter?
Stay their place did the last fearsome fighters

Although Demons quake the world, footsteps Thunder
She only laughs at the mask of the Eternal Slumber

Smiling, eager to show her ways
Soon her strength covered all as the sun's rays

Glory, glory be to all your days
Oh glory be with you

The Sorceress

Thrace

<u>Unworthy</u>

The armies stand ready
Archers, their bows held steady
Each man, spear heeled, brow sweaty
Heart pounding upon their chests, all levied

Families cower in their kingdoms
"Favor our sons!" to The One, praying

War drums sound
The ground trembles

As they march and shout
Raging embers spout

Enough

To the middle I leap and land
Crushing boulders into sand

I cry out to my enemies
"Give me your strongest champion!
Let us settle this!"

A moment passes

Aria Rozo

I stretch my wrists
Whiten my knuckles
Though a giant will come,
I will not buckle

Soon, a figure rises
A man, small in stature
Yet I see in his shadowed eyes,
A fiery nature

He runs to me, and leaps
I smile, grip my hammer and swing

Quickly, he dodges
His blades and my flesh meet

Blood flows freely outwards
As I grip his leg, and slam him downwards

Only briefly stunned, he twists
I let go, a swing missed

Jumping away, he throws knives
Into my muscles, they are buried
Yet I ignore them, my hammer split in two
I strike enraged, in fury

With daggers, he tries to parry my blows
But I only treat them as toys for show

Ending my enemy I stand victorious
The clouds Cirrus
My armies roar,
Only one death, their spirits soar

Yet as I gaze at the man's body
Its familiarity puts me in worry

Weakness I cannot show, yet I collapse
My helmet fails to hide my gasp

A wind passes the ground below,
I see now, I reap what I sowed

Fluttering, like wings of a sparrow
The cloth, covering the face, reveals my sorrow

My enemy's eyes were not a man's

But the jewels of my precious Yarrow

Aria Rozo

The Fall

<u>The Maiden</u>

Unwrap me
The unwanted gift
Your cursed belonging, veil lift

Sin
Lost in the sheltered forests
Artificial ruin

Come, see
Why have the Winds tamed you?
Cool your breaths as they pass
Each one, more empty than the past

Come, unsheathe me
Be not afraid of your power
A Sword to life you cut
Bleed, inch to death, your Wrath

Throw me,
Burning into the pyre
Mists of spark, soul the air
Soar higher

Fight me
Struggle against your Lusts,
The waves that toppled your Paradise
Fly ere it crumbles

Share me,
No, give, you must
Faster!

Seal this torment upon The Latter
Only the Storm can now Break your Fetters

In Her Stead

I kneel beside you
The rain pours, parting
Water mixes with red, two
I unwrap this blanket, my wing

The one you made me with great Sacrifice
Cover your body, Warmth empty
I grip your hands, clenched tightly
I stand at the precipice

Before the Tomb of the Zenith
Can The One truly make it?

I call out to the Heavens
Let my voice ring, penetrate the silence

Uncomposed I am now
Disheveled in this struggle
I care not for my pride
Nothing lingers
All cast cast aside

In my strength I never bowed
Only others pleaded
But now I cry out for mercy
The King on the other Side seated

"Take me!"
I wait for an answer

"Take me in her stead!"
The storm only grows colder

"I care not if I suffer!"
Willingly I would give my soul

"Let me alone bear all of Hell!"
No price is too much, no Toll

I fall down, my knees on the ground
My forehead upon the sand, to desperation bound

Yet no sunlight pours through
Only cruel slander

As I gaze upon
This broken Flower

Senna

Senna, oh Senna
Back turned, a calming sight
Warm smells of a kitchen, this morning bright
Sounds of children playing, shaking the rafters
Our bellies filled with both hot soup and laughter

Senna, oh Senna
'Round the table all gather
Your voice booms, the gentle mother
Prayer sated, hands grasp bread awaited
Ale sipped, calm thirst, lips elated

Senna, oh Senna
Worry not, my armor is sound
Off I am, battle bound

Open door, my step halted
You hold me, the children's cries lilted

Senna, oh Senna
The others call
I leave this necklace
And with each a kiss
I am here always
Do not, me, miss

Senna, oh Senna
Soon I will come home, no tarry
I will return this letter, calm your worry
Boom as they will, we will survive the enemy
Our minds are strong

Our last stand is ready.

Night Rainbow

The moon shining
A night rainbow

Hello halo
Hello

The road curves
Goodbye

A misty breath
Alibi

If you called me
I would answer

If you held me
I would cry

See the life I've taken
Our feet curls at the shaking

This bed is our backyard
This bed is our fire

A double meaning
The steam rises

Your soup fills me
In your eyes, I see in

Grip me   .
I sin

My body is yours
Yours is mine

A unity of separation

Creation

Sublime

Fear of Life

"I'm scared." whispered the ghost
"Hold me." the grip tightened. "Come close."

"Beyond is so dark. I cannot see."
The Hunter laid down the book and took pity.

She smiled.

Finally, a listener.
"Thank you."

"What troubles you?" he asked the prisoner.

"Centuries have passed, yet my thoughts are the same.
In my sadness, I do not my killer blame."
She floated to her remains.

"I was to become great, a singer of tales.
Yet my time was stolen,
Not ending when I was frail."

The Hunter sit and his cigar lit.
The ghost asked
"What troubles you?
Who breaks your wit?"

"You.
No ghost is this friendly."
He glanced at his book
Shook his canteen

"My regret lies
In losing my family."
Taking a drink, he coughed
And spilled it on the ground
A pool, reflecting a strange sheen

"Now you seek revenge,
For the life that was taken
The life you would have lived
Had their bodies not been broken."

He chuckled to himself
And stood coughing
The ghost was puzzled, but remained quiet.

"The manner angers me more.
Bodies strewn upon the floor.
The whole house was to Hell a door."

He took a puff and sat still.
"Only four knew The End."

He looked at his cigar.

"Now there is only one more."

Silence entered
A cold gust whispered.

She laughed to herself.
"Thank you for listening, mister."

He dropped his cigar and reached for the book
But the ghost was faster, and his body took.

They struggled for some time, shaking the floor
The cigar rolled until
It caught the alcohol

The ghost killed his soul, refreshed in the new world
Yet now she understood why her new vessel twirls

The fires consumed both her and him
But still neither screamed

Many say they fear when the lights go dim

Yet it terrifies more how they lived

Aria Rozo

Her

Look down upon your children
Have mercy upon the cursed stricken

They have been entranced by Her beauty
The fair maiden
Immortal
Bitten

Day and night they conspire to meet her
A secret so hidden they themselves do not notice

Their hands move to caress her
Tempted, they embrace
Take in shared breaths
Evermore entwisted fates

They proclaim love for Her
Although the path shall lead to ruin
They will keep holding

They offer their blood and tears
The ground tastes none
No, not in any year

Have mercy Father upon the bane
Your Creation and Destruction the same

Aria Rozo

When She's Gone

I lay and watch clouds
Your warm smile
Black hair dancing about

Your hold surrounds
I calm
Your sweet humming
My vision, sound

Now I stand
Across the mountains
Love conquers distance
But I will what they won't give admittance

I always lived as a young man would
Strong and proud
I don't need you
I could...

Yet, I dreamt
And I awoke

It was no dream
Now I'm the joke

You're gone.

I'm alone.

Aria Rozo

The Stay

Something Beautiful

The mirror shatters
Just how much courage can I muster?

Color, I paint your eyes
Yet with words, I want to fill what inside lies

I run out words

So I ran

Rain falls,
I beg for clues

Yet, as I travel through water pools
My soul flies away
To Heaven?
No, Hell

Aria Rozo

This is Purgatory.
Let my heart pour

Now I see,
These words are not for you
But for me

Comfort, I run towards but do not seek
Pain and struggle, I flee from but need

Beauty is my desire
From the brutal truth I cry, yet do not tire

I stop atop the Bridge to my Death
Gaze, watch with bated breaths
Finally, I have found my rest

Let me make you something beautiful

Lullaby

Yes, you uttered
My heart, oh how it fluttered

The butterflies cross the sky
The shrubbery of red petal
Their scent and sparkle, shy

My lungs fill
Your palms upon mine lay still

The scars of birth run your cheek
Did the treasure of smiles
Bring enough to stop your seek?

Enough

The closing of eyes is enough

Too long have mine remained open

Too much has your love been stripped naked

The trickle of the stream, the river
Your blood like wine, it delivers

The mouth of the Evil one opens
She drinks

None

Beauty and madness a blessed sin
The gods betray you, the final win

Peace and forgiveness, once, did you mean
Gone now, the Source
Wolfed down, stripped clean

Choose what's chosen
Mirror what's spoken
Their Words you embrace emblazoned

Just as the fire rises
All in the dark is revealed

Inside lies the libertine

You were never free to begin

Sparks, into air float
Disappearing in a final grace

Walk, the stones your feet cut in
Run, the dust medicine

From whence we were Once born
We shall soon, Two, return

Upon the field of flowers our hands once combed
We will fall, justly entombed

Do not worry
It ends not in this day

This lullaby is only for
Paradise

The final Stay

Aria Rozo

Homeless Man

Why do you avert your eyes?
Fear to cross gazes
Why do you move away with haste?
I have no malicious intent

You wander at my cars
I tell you, I have nowhere to go
You covet my mistresses
I tell you, I am cold every night
You drool at my dinner table
I tell you, I have no appetite
You envy my palace

I tell you, I have no home.

At this moment, you stand
You think me worthy of honor
The honor to be called a Man
Yet I tell you, I am still a Boy

Can you hear my plead?
Under all these costumes?
Can you not see me suffocate?

Perhaps I am already dead.

It has always been business
This life

I paid them my Debts
Many years ago
Tenfold their life's sacrifice
I gave in a day
Tenfold of what they hoped I would be
I am

Yet still

This is not my home...
I never had one

Nor I ever will.

Don't Stay Here

Turn away, run
Do not stay here

Your whispers hit me,
Unseen, a dark sun

Darkness now I do not fear
The cool night air bites me,
The winds, shears

I embrace willingly, the numb
But my mind is rampant, soul none

Run, do not stay here

The chimes they betray us
Hold fast, come the gust

I am your past, I know
Your future, there, another

Go
Run, you must
Do not stay here...

The winds shatter the water glass
Drops fall down, but it rains not

The voice I yearn for threads my conscious
Sewing together a fate not obvious

Is it not enough to say we've tried?
How much will it cost to give more and survive?

The light of your shadow pierces my steady gaze
Through the smoke, I cough, a deep haze

Run, do not stay here

Run, your presence incites fear

Fear of senescence,
Any other punishment is of a lesser sentence

Run, do not stay here...

I loved you, and perhaps I continue to

But that has passed, or my mind, thinks it so...

Run...

Don't.

Stay here.

All Is One Yet Separate

All is one, yet separate.
The light from the deepest darkness, dies not in any fight.
The silence is never drowned by the loudest calls.
From nothingness springs forth everything in sight.

Just as the dawn is no different from the stilled twilight.
And like a thought, the maker of the world, is shaped by the known stranger,
Fate
Everything changes, yet this quality is the only constant.
As the multitude grows, the faces disappear
Yet the one name of all becomes known
Man

Tears from pain will continue to be dreary.
But when shed in cheer, they become a bounty.

The Light is no longer, without the Dark.
And if Life is a heavy blessing, it cannot be so without the releasing Death.

The stairway to Heaven is Hell.
For the same Hand that heals a mistake,
Punishes to prevent another, a way One fell

For the sacrifice of The Mother
Though is makes Her life harder
Benefits Her Children, and thereafter
Gives Her a chance for freeing laughter

Open your eyes to take it all, blessing and sin
Then close them, to receive Peace within
Own and you will be owned
This is the greatest tragedy

But let go...

And though all will pass by, bitter sweetly
In the end
You will smile, if only for a little while

Hope

Faith

Love

It is the same here
As it is above.

Here, Hear

Listening to the silence
Watching her move through the darkness
Feeling the air move about the room
My senses are full

Yet I cannot forget about the impending doom

For just a moment, we are here alone
For just a time, we are free

In these passing moments, I know

The world knows

She is still living

No.

She lives

Aria Rozo

End

Adieu

The glass is full

Where there is no water
There is air
Even if they forget
It is still there

I look around me
Where are you
Papers filled with writing
At your portraits do I stare

I see you
This room is full

I walk about
The dust dancing
The sunlight pours

Never did you say

Adieu

Aria Rozo

Out There

She looked to the starry skies and pondered
As they drifted through celestial wonder

Outside these windows, she could imagine
Worlds of new color she could run in

A place far away from home
Ravaged by those with hearts of stone

Perhaps in this empty space they drift
They could find a place untold
Where the sun is brightly shining
And flowers bloom in the cold

Indeed, peace they would forge
Only love

No more hate to gorge
Untethered doves

She leans on her hands
Sinks into slumber

Yes, perhaps there is a world like that
Somewhere out there...

Aria Rozo

The Land of the Immortals

In the land of the Immortals
The people are free
And good intentions
All come to be

Every war brings life
Blood is only given,
Not drawn by knives
Saved are the sickened

Death is a gift
There is bounty in mourning
Their lives are celebrated
As they wake to another morning

Vast fields of wheat
The children run and soar
As the Rulers serve and feed
No one yearns for more

In the land of the Immortals
The sun is the shade
Set upon gentle waters the people sleep
Their beds rocked by waves

In the land of the Immortals
The people are free
All fear drowned out by the inner courage
That has come out to be...

Me

Aria Rozo

Again

Atop the mountain, the small flower shies
Just as the hues of Dawn change, its colors lie

For the Hidden refuse to leave the cling of Night,
Its colds sky's might, comfort found in dark light

Yet their beauty remains cast, lit
Like a memory of the filtered past
Forgotten, but lingering
The taste of the Aurea lasts

If again
I could hold it
My soul I would give to keep

For the soft flutters of your presence
Moves the air about me, gone its senescence

Goodbye, Once more
Life I've never seen

Let me soon

Again

FOREWORD

Perhaps there are riddles

We can never truly solve

Some questions, the only answers

To the Loves we truly hold

I look to the Heavens

Upon the powers that once made me

My shadows pierce the blaze

My voice now recalls

———

Index

The

The Halcyon Days

The Calm

The Climb

The Storm

The Fall

The Stay

End

www.ingramcontent.com/pod-product-compliance
Lightning Source LLC
Chambersburg PA
CBHW071908020426
42331CB00010B/2720